# THE CHEETAH

## THE BIG CAT DISCOVERY LIBRARY

Lynn M. Stone

Rourke Enterprises, Inc.
Vero Beach, Florida 32964

PHOTO CREDITS
© Lynn M. Stone: Pages 1, 4, 7, 8, 12, 13, 15, 18, 21, and
cover; © Ahup and Manoj Shah/ Animals Animals: Page 10;
© Joe McDonald/Animals Animals: Page 17


ACKNOWLEDGEMENTS

The author wishes to thank the following for special
photographic assistance in the preparation of this book:
Cincinnati Zoo
FOR CATHERINE HILKER AND ANGEL,
A VERY SPECIAL CHEETAH


**Library of Congress Cataloging-in-Publication Date**
Stone, Lynn M.
    Cheetahs / Lynn M. Stone.
    p. cm. — (The big cat discovery library)
    Includes index.
    Summary: An introduction to the physical characteristics,
habits, natural environment, relationship to humans, and
future of the cheetah, the big, spotted cat that is the fastest
mammal on earth.
    ISBN 0-86592-503-8
    1. Cheetahs—Juvenile literature [1. Cheetahs.] I. Title.
II. Series: Stone, Lynn M. Big cat discovery library.
QL737.C23S765 1989            89-32643
599.74'428—dc20                   CIP
                                            AC

# TABLE OF CONTENTS

# THE CHEETAH

The cheetah *(Acinonyx jubatus)* is not a bird or a plane, but it almost flies. This big, spotted cat is the fastest mammal on earth. Its bursts of speed reach 70 miles per hour. Because of its bounding run, its feet are actually off the ground for half the distance it races.

Unlike a horse, which can gallop up to 43 miles per hour, a wild cheetah doesn't run for sport. A cheetah runs for its dinner.

A cheetah can run at top speed for only about three-tenths of a mile. If it fails to catch the animal it's chasing, it must stop to catch its breath. Later, when rested, the cheetah will hunt again.

*Cheetah*

## THE CHEETAH'S COUSINS

The cheetah has been called the "hunting leopard". Cheetahs are related to leopards and all cats, or **felines**. But cheetahs are the most "un-catlike" of the whole cat family.

Among other things, the claws, teeth, and skulls of cheetahs are different from those of other cats. Cheetah claws, for instance, are not hidden, nor are they sharply curved as they are in other cats. The pads on their feet are small and tough, like a dog's. Their legs and paws are slim, and their bodies are amazingly flexible. Rather than stalk **prey** in cat fashion, cheetahs, like dogs, run after animals they want to eat.

There are as many as eight different types of cheetahs. All are closely related.

*Cheetah Paws*

## HOW THEY LOOK

Male cheetahs weigh about 125 pounds, the same as many spotted leopards. Cheetahs, however, are taller and much slimmer than leopards. They have small, dome-like heads. Their long legs look like they were borrowed from a greyhound.

Cheetahs have yellowish or cream-colored fur freckled with black spots. The spots on a few African cheetahs blend into stripes.

Cheetahs have dark, deep-set eyes and black stripes that travel like tears from their inner eye corners to their mouth.

Like a greyhound, a cheetah has a deep chest that contains large lungs and a powerful heart. These organs help the cat to run at high speed.

*Cheetah Tear Stripes*

## WHERE THEY LIVE

Until recently the cheetah lived in parts of Africa and in such Asian nations as Iraq, Iran, Russia, and India. Today the cheetah still lives in several African countries. However, it may be **extinct** outside of Africa. That means that the cheetahs in Asia may have all disappeared. Some scientists think that a few cheetahs may still live in Iran, but no one is sure.

Cheetah **habitats**, or homes, are the open spaces. They like the grassland, desert-like plains, and brush country of Africa. Cheetahs do not like forests. Trees stop them from using their speed.

In Africa, cheetahs are found in many of the same national parks as their cousins, leopards and lions.

*Cheetah on Ant Hill, Kenya*

Cheetah

## HOW THEY LIVE

Cheetahs live their lives in the fast lane. Although most big cats spend a great deal of time at rest, cheetahs usually have to hunt every second or third day.

Cheetahs are not only busy hunters, but they also have to be quick eaters. They do not climb well, so they can not stash a kill in a tree like the leopard can. They are too slender to defend their food against other hunters, such as lions, wild dogs, hyenas, and leopards. Therefore cheetahs must eat quickly, and fiercer animals often force them to leave part of their meal.

Cheetahs spend some time in groups. Males even hunt together, but not with as much skill as lions that hunt together.

*Cheetah Running*

# THE CHEETAH'S CUBS

A cheetah's **litter** averages four cubs. The babies are blind for about one week. The mother raises them on her milk and on meat from her kills. A cheetah mother has to kill prey almost every day for her fluffy gray cubs.

At the age of three months, the cubs no longer depend on milk. They are spotted now, no longer gray, and they begin to follow their mother. By watching her, they learn to hunt.

One-year old cheetahs kill some of their own prey. They leave their mother three or four months later as young adults.

Cheetahs in zoos rarely live more than 10 years. In the wild, the average life span is even shorter.

# PREDATOR AND PREY

Among themselves, cheetahs can be very playful and friendly. But cheetahs are **predators**—hunters. At hunting time, cheetahs become deadly serious.

Cheetahs have excellent vision. They scan the plains for a likely victim. Unlike other cats, a cheetah does not sneak carefully toward its prey. It runs after prey. The cheetah knocks the animal down and grabs it by the throat.

Cheetahs kill many different animals. Small antelope, like gazelles, are a favorite prey.

Cheetahs do not hide their kill for another day. They aren't strong enough to drag a large animal into hiding. They eat where they kill, and circling vultures often give away the place to other predators.

Cheetahs, especially the cubs, can be prey for lions and leopards.

*Cheetah Prey: Gazelles*

# CHEETAHS AND PEOPLE

For centuries, people tamed and trained cheetahs to hunt for them. The use of cheetahs as trained hunters is called **coursing**. It used to be popular in Egypt, India, and even in Europe. The practice may have begun 5,000 years ago.

Tame cheetahs purr and enjoy human attention. Coursers used to prefer them to dogs as hunting companions. Unlike the other big cats, cheetahs are normally not dangerous to people.

Cheetahs are beautiful, and people enjoy seeing them in zoos. Now the problem of captive cheetahs dying young may have been solved. Research at the Cincinnati Zoo has shown that too much vitamin A in the food of captive cheetahs was slowly killing them. Cheetah diets have been changed.

# THE CHEETAH'S FUTURE

Only a small portion of Africa is good habitat for cheetahs, and some of that is being turned into farms. No animal can live without proper habitat.

Killing cheetahs is against the law in most African countries, but **poachers**, people who break hunting laws, kill them anyway. The cheetah's spotted coat is very valuable.

Some African farmers also kill cheetahs. The cheetahs, they say, frighten antelope and zebra herds from their property.

Cheetahs need more large **preserves** where they can live safely. Without them, the 10,000 to 15,000 remaining African cheetahs may face the same fate as the Asian cheetah—extinction.

# Glossary

**coursing** (KOR sing)—the use of hunting animals, such as cheetahs, to chase other animals

**extinct** (ex TINKT)—no longer existing

**feline** (FEE line)—any of the cats

**habitat** (HAB a tat)—the area in which an animal lives

**litter** (LIT er)—a group of baby animals born of the same mother at the same time

**poacher** (PO cher)—someone who hunts animals against the law

**predator** (PRED a tor)—an animal that kills other animals for food

**preserve** (pre ZERV)—an area where wild animals are protected from man

**prey** (PRAY)—an animal that is hunted for food by another animal

# INDEX